THE
SALADS
COOKBOOK

100 Delicious, Creative & Exquisite Salad Recipes To Enjoy.

OLLIE TURNER

Copyright © 2015 by Ollie Turner. All rights reserved

Copyright

All rights reserved. No part of this publication may be reproduced, distributed, or transmitted in any form or by any means, including photocopying, recording, or other electronic or mechanical methods, without the prior written permission of the publisher, except in the case of brief quotations embodied in critical reviews and certain other non-commercial uses permitted by copyright law.

Legal Disclaimer

The information in the book is for educational purposes only. It is not medical advice and is not intended to replace the advice or attention of health-care professionals. Consult your physician before beginning or making any changes in your diet. Specific medical advice should be obtained from a licensed health-care practitioner. Ollie Turner and his associates will not assume any liability, nor be held responsible for any injury, illness or personal loss due to the utilization of any information contained herein.

CONTENTS

WELCOME	7
WHAT MAKES A GOOD SALAD?	8
VEGETARIAN FRIENDLY SALADS	13
SEAFOOD & FISH SALADS	45
MEATY SALADS	65
DRESSINGS	97

WELCOME

Firstly I'd like to thank you for purchasing my book – The Salads Cookbook.

Over the last couple of years, salads seem to have got a bad rap. They seem to be only associated with super skinny models on diets along with the latest fads. However salads done correctly are tasty, filling and beautiful too.

In my opinion, this book contains the most creative, satisfying and delicious salads… ever!

Every recipe included in this cookbook is easy to follow and even easier to prepare. You'll figure out that you don't have to be master chef or cooking whizz to make beautiful, exciting, tasty salads that you can enjoy any time.

Let's get started!

Ollie Turner

WHAT MAKES A GREAT SALAD?

Salads are not only healthy - they're delicious too! If you aren't already a salad lover, prepare to be converted. Whether you have bought this cookbook to lose weight, try some more variety in the salad world, or simply just because you think salad is great, this is the book for you.

The top secrets to making delicious salads are all combined in the recipes that follow but if you want to continue eating amazing salads then the following secrets will ensure that each and every salad you prepare for yourself, your family, or your friends will be amazing.

TOP SECRET 1: SALADS DON'T HAVE TO BE FIT FOR A RABBIT.

Lettuce is a key essential in most salads, but iceberg doesn't have to be the only bed you lay your ingredients on: try a range of lettuce leaves and experiment with mixing them. Rocket, spinach, watercress, lamb's, cos… the list goes on. Additionally, lettuce is not the only thing you need use to bulk out your recipes. Switch it up for unusual alternatives – try grated carrots, celeriac, cabbage, grains including couscous, barley, quinoa.

TOP SECRET 2: ORGANIC, LOCAL AND SEASONAL INGREDIENTS ARE ALWAYS SUPERIOR.

If you can get hold of ingredients that fit the above bill then you must. Salads always tastw best using the food that can be found at the time of eating. Hence why we tend to eat more in the summer. Needless to say there are salads fit for autumn and winter, but try to stick to those ingredients that haven't been shipped/airfreighted in. Not only will it taste better but you will feel better too, knowing you're doing the right thing for the world and for your stomach.

TOP SECRET 3: HOMEMADE SALAD DRESSINGS ARE BETTER

Don't waste money buying jars and bottles of your favourite dressings. They're often full of preservatives, extra calories AND you spend more money on the convenience. That's without mentioning the wasted plastic and glass used to contain them. Homemade dressings are delicious and healthy and you can season and adjust to your own taste. A bottle of olive oil, balsamic vinegar, red wine vinegar and simple seasonings are all you really need as a base for most dressings.

TOP SECRET 4: DON'T BE SCARED TO EXPERIMENT

Because you're creating the salads at home you can afford to throw in your favourite foods and flavours. Use these recipes as a base and inspiration and continue your salad making skills by combining all of your favourite things. Hint: different textures work well in a salad to give you that crunch and smoothness and keep you intrigued.

TOP SECRET 5: FLAVOUR, FLAVOUR, FLAVOUR!

Use spices, citrus and fresh herbs to top off your salad with that extra special touch. Fresh ingredients make people smile and citrus from lemons and limes and even oranges can really bring out the flavours of the main ingredients in your salad. Don't neglect your main ingredients however: make sure meat and fish is cooked through properly; if it should be served cold allow to cool completely before adding to the salad base; blend cheeses and fruits with the meats to diversify.

VEGETARIAN FRIENDLY SALADS

Whilst salads are not the only choice for vegetarians they are a scrumptious go-to. That being said, vegetarian salads are tasty whether you like to eat meat or not. These recipes are all suitable for vegetarians just make sure that the cheese you purchase is definitely not made with animal rennet (I have not included those cheeses known for this such as parmesan and gorgonzola).

Fresh and healthy ideas, these recipes are superb shared with friends and family on a summer's evening, made to accompany any dinner, or as a lunchtime treat to keep you going.

SCRUMPTIOUS SPINACH & GLORIOUS WATERCRESS SALAD

Ingredients

- 70g of Spinach
- 70g of Watercress
- 70g of Rocket
- 3 tsp of Olive Oil
- 1 tsp of red wine vinegar
- Handful of flaked almonds
- 60g of raisins
- Dash of black pepper
- Dash of salt

How to make:

- Mix the olive oil, vinegar and seasoning in a large salad bowl. Add the salad leaves, raisins and almonds and toss thoroughly. Serve ASAP!

DELECTABLE AVOCADO SALAD

Ingredients

- 1 large chopped avocado (chopped into large pieces)
- 6 chopped lettuce leaves
- 8 halved cherry tomatoes
- 3 diced radishes
- 1 diced cucumber
- Handful of chopped parsley leaves
- Handful of chopped mint leaves
- Salt
- Pepper
- 1 tbsp of lemon juice
- 2 tbsp of olive oil
- 1 crushed garlic clove
- Pinch of salt
- Pinch of pepper

How to make:

- Mix the lemon juice, olive oil, salt, pepper and garlic clove together. Leave to one side. Add all the salad ingredients to a bowl and season with some salt and pepper and mix together thoroughly. Add the dressing just before serving!

GORGEOUS GREEN GEM SALAD

Ingredients

- 8 Baby Gem lettuce leaves
- 2 tsp of white wine vinegar
- 1 finely sliced red onion
- 120g of finely sliced radishes
- 1 tbsp of olive oil
- Half an orange

How to make:

- Mix the white wine vinegar and olive oil together before squeezing the juice from the orange into the mix as well. Add the salad ingredients to a bowl and drizzle with the orange mixture. Serve.

DIVINE FETA, CHICORY & POMEGRANATE SALAD

Ingredients

- 150g of crumbled feta cheese
- 1 halved, pomegranate seeds
- 4 chicory
- 1 tbsp of red wine vinegar
- 3 tbsp of olive oil
- 85g of watercress (stalks removed)
- Salt
- Pepper

How to make:

- In a salad bowl, add the salad leaves and pomegranate seeds. Whisk together the olive oil, vinegar, salt and pepper together to make the dressing. Drizzle the dressing over the salad along with the crumbled feta. Toss and serve ASAP.

MOZZARELLA AND TOMATO BABY SPINACH SALAD

Ingredients

- 100g of diced mozzarella
- 100g of baby spinach leaves
- 1 diced yellow pepper
- 100g of sun dried tomatoes
- 2 tbsp of sun dried tomato oil or Olive oil
- 2 tsp of balsamic vinegar
- 2 tsp of pumpkin seeds
- 1 finely chopped cucumber
- Salt
- Pepper

How to make:

- Get a large bowl and add the tomatoes, spinach leaves, yellow pepper and chopped cucumber in a bowl and toss together. Add the mozzarella to the bowl and sprinkle with the pumpkin seeds. Finally drizzle the vinegar over the salad along with the tomato oil. Serve immediately.

YUMMY HAZELNUT AND ORANGE SALAD

Ingredients

- 150g of baby spinach leaves
- 3 peeled oranges
- 85g of chopped, toasted hazelnuts
- 100g of cooked green beans
- 200g of cooked chopped beetroot
- 3 tbsp of olive oil
- 2 tbsp of honey
- 2 tbsp of white wine vinegar

How to make:

- Add all the salad ingredients to a bowl and toss thoroughly. Whisk together the honey, vinegar and olive oil together and drizzle over the salad.

LEMONY ROCKET & FENNEL SALAD

Ingredients

- 200g of rocket
- 3 thinly sliced and cored fennel bulbs
- 1 thinly sliced red onion
- Zest and juice of 1 lemon
- 4 tbsp of olive oil
- Salt
- Pepper

How to make:

- Mix together the oil, lemon juice, salt and pepper. In a bowl add the salad ingredients and lemon zest and toss. Drizzle the lemony oil over the salad and serve.

DOLCELATTE & WALNUT SALAD

Ingredients

- 75g dolcelatte cheese
- 60g of walnuts
- 120g of baby spinach leaves
- 3 tbsp of crème fraîche
- Sprinkle of salt
- Sprinkle of pepper

How to make:

- Mix the crème fraîche, cheese, salt and pepper with 40 ml of water in a bowl. Mix until smooth. Add the spinach to a salad bowl, sprinkle over the walnut pieces. Finally drizzle the dressing over the salad and serve.

TANGY CARROT & AVOCADO SALAD

Ingredients

- 4 halved and sliced carrots
- 100g of rocket leaves
- 2 sliced, peeled and stoned avocados
- 1 tbsp of olive oil
- Juice and zest of 1 orange

How to make:

- Add the carrots, rocket and half of the orange into the bowl. In a small bowl, mix the zest, oil and squeeze the juice from the other half of the orange in. Drizzle over the salad and toss.

GOATS CHEESE AND LAMB LETTUCE SALAD

Ingredients

- 100g of crumbled goat's cheese
- 100g of lamb's lettuce
- 50g of walnuts
- 1 chopped shallot
- 1 tbsp of olive oil
- 1 tsp of red wine vinegar

How to make:

- Add all the salad ingredients to a salad bowl and toss thoroughly. Sprinkle over the goats cheese and serve.

GRECIAN SALAD

Ingredients

- 100g of iceberg lettuce
- 6 large halved vine tomatoes
- 1 chopped cucumber
- 1 thinly sliced red onion
- 18 black olives
- 50g of diced feta cheese
- 3 tbsp of olive oil
- 1 tsp of dried oregano

How to make:

- Add all the ingredients to a bowl and toss thoroughly. Sprinkle with salt and pepper and serve.

SWEET POMEGRANATE & NUT SALAD

Ingredients

- 75g of pomegranate seeds
- 75g of chopped walnuts
- 25g of baby spinach
- 25g of rocket
- 25g of lettuce
- 4 tbsp of red wine vinegar
- Small handful of chopped dill
- Small handful of chopped mint
- Handful of chopped spring onions
- 1 tbsp of clear honey
- Zest and juice of 1 orange

How to make:

- Get a bowl and mix the zest, juice and honey with some salt and pepper. Add the rest of the ingredients to a large salad bowl. Pour the juice mixture evenly over the salad, toss and serve immediately.

HEAVENLY COURGETTE, POPPY SEED & SPINACH SALAD

Ingredients

- 3 grated courgettes
- 2 tbsp of olive oil
- Handful of baby spinach leaves
- 1 tbsp of lime juice
- 1 tbsp of clear honey
- 3 tbsp of poppy seeds
- 1 crushed garlic clove

How to make:

- Add all the ingredients to a large salad bowl and toss thoroughly. Sprinkle some salt and pepper over the salad to finish.

EPIC HALLOUMI, WILD ROCKET & COUSCOUS SALAD

Ingredients

- 200g of cooked couscous
- 200g of sliced and charred halloumi chesse
- 75g of wild rocket (normal rocket is fine)
- 100g of drained and rinsed chickpeas
- 75ml of natural greek yogurt
- 25g of sundried tomatoes
- 3 diced red peppers
- 2tbsp of harissa

How to make:

- Mix the yogurt and harissa together. In a salad bowl, add the chickpeas, sundried tomatoes, wild rocket, couscous and red peppers and toss thoroughly. Add the halloumi and drizzle the salad with the yogurt.

CHERRY TOMATO, SPRING ONION & AVOCADO SALAD

Ingredients

- 8 halved cherry tomatoes
- 4 diced spring onions
- 1 chopped avocado
- 2 tbsp of olive oil
- 1 crushed garlic clove
- 4 chopped lamb lettuce leaves
- 2 chopped Cos lettuce leaves
- 25g of chopped mint leaves
- 35g of chopped parsley leaves
- 2 tbsp of lemon juice
- Salt
- Pepper

How to make:

- Mix the garlic, lemon juice and olive oil together with some salt. Add of the other ingredients to a large salad bowl. Drizzle the dressing over the salad along with some pepper and toss thoroughly.

SUNDRIED TOMATO, BULGHAR WHEAT AND AUBERGINE SALAD

Ingredients

- 200g of pre cooked bulghar wheat
- 1 jar of sundried tomatoes and oil from the jar
- 6 sliced aubergines
- 2 tbsp of olive oil
- 2 diced red peppers
- Handful of rocket
- Handful of basil leaves
- Salt
- Pepper

How to make

- Pre heat a griddle pan to a high heat and add the aubergines along with the peppers and some olive oil and cook for 10 minutes, turning the aubergines over half way through until lightly charred. Remove the aubergines from the pan and place to one side.
- In a bowl, mix the bulghar wheat, sundried tomatoes and oil from the jar together. Add the aubergines, red peppers, some salt and pepper, rocket and the basil leaves. Toss and serve.

BUTTER BEAN, CANNELLINI BEAN & SPRING ONION SALAD

Ingredients

- 200g of butter beans
- 600g of drained and rinsed cannellini beans
- 2 handfuls of chopped spring onions
- 7 tbsp of olive oul
- 2 crushed garlic cloves
- Handful of chopped parsley
- 2 tbsp of white whine vinegar
- 2 chopped and seeded red chilli's
- Handful of rocket

How to make:

- In a large salad bowl, mix all the ingredients together and sprinkle a decent amount of salt and pepper over the top.

LEMONY AVOCADO WITH CHIVES AND ROCKET SALAD

Ingredients

- 200g of rocket
- 4 tbsp of olive oil
- 2 diced avocados
- 2 tbsp of lemon juice
- 1 spinkle of salt
- Handful of finely chopped chives

How to make:

- Mix the lemon juice, salt, olive oil and chives together. Add the rocket and avocados to a bowl and drizzle with the dressing. Toss and serve

PEELED COURGETTE, BABY SPINACH & CRUMBLED FETA SALAD

Ingredients

- 3 peeled courgettes
- 50g of baby spinach
- 50g of rocket
- 150g of crumbled feta cheese
- Handful of chopped mint leaves
- 2 tbsp of olive oil
- Salt
- Pepper

How to make:

- Add all of the ingredients into a salad bowl, drizzle with the olive oil, toss and serve.

DELICIOUS GREEN BEAN SALAD

Ingredients

- 200 of baby spinach
- 100g of lamb's lettuce
- Juice of 1 lemon
- 500g of fine green beans
- 3 tbsp of olive oil

How to make:

- To make the dressing, mix the olive oil and lemon juice along with some salt and pepper together. In a large salad bowl, mix the spinach, lettuce and green beans together. Drizzle over the dressing and serve.

BEAUTIFUL BABY NEW POTATO SALAD

Ingredients

- 350g of boiled baby new potatoes
- Handful of rocket
- 2 tsp of Dijon mustard
- 4 tbsp of olive oil
- Zest and juice from 1 lemon
- 4 tbsp of chopped parsley
- 3 diced spring onions

How to make:

- Mix the mustard, lemon zest, lemon juice and olive oil together. To serve and the potatoes to a bowl along with the dressing and mix together. Finish off by adding the parsley, spring onions and rocket to the bowl.

CARROT, CHOPPED CASHEW AND FENNEL SALAD

Ingredients

- 3 grated carrots
- 3 thinly sliced fennel bulbs
- Handful of lightly toasted cashew nuts
- 2 tbsp of olive oil
- Juice and zest of 1 lime
-

How to make:

- Add all the ingredients to a large salad bowl and toss thoroughly.

POWERFUL AVOCADO & WATERCRESS LEAF SALAD

Ingredients

- 3 peeled, stoned and chopped avocados
- 50g of watercress
- 25g of rocket
- 25g of baby spinach
- 75g of ready made croutons
- 2 tsp of Dijon mustard
- 1 tbsp of white wine vinegar
- 3 tbsp of olive oil
- Salt
- Pepper

How to make:

- To make the dressing, add the mustard, white wine vinegar, oil and a tbsp. of water together. Season with some salt and pepper.
- Get a large salad bowl and add of the other ingredients (apart from the croutons) along with the dressing and toss thoroughly. Add the croutons and serve

FENNEL, ROCKET & PINE NUT SALAD

Ingredients

- 100g of toasted pine nuts
- 100g of rocket
- 1 thinly sliced head of fennel
- 3 tbsp of olive oil
- Juice of 1 orange

How to make:

- In a large salad bowl mix all the ingredients together and toss thoroughly.

CUTE CHERRY, BEAN & RED ONION SALAD

Ingredients

- 800g of drained and rinsed cannellini beans
- 100g of halved cherry tomatoes
- 1 thinly sliced red onion
- 2 tbsp red wine vinegar
- Handful of chopped basil leaves

How to make:

- Mix everything together in a large bowl. Add some salt and pepper and just before serving, add the basil.

TASTY PESTO TORTELLINI & BROCCOLI TENDERSTEM SALAD

Ingredients

- 225g of tortellini
- 120g of diced tenderstem broccoli
- 3 tbsp of pesto (vegetarian friendly so avoid the ones with parmesan or alternatively make your own with fresh basil, cheddar cheese, pine nuts and olive oil whizzed up in a blender)
- 3 tbsp od toasted pine nuts
- 1 tbsp of balsamic vinegar
- 10 halved cherry tomatoes

How to make:

- Get a large pan of water and place on a high eat until the water boils. Add the broccoli to the pan and leave to boil for 2 minutes. Add the tortellini and cook according to packet instructions. Drain the pan and then tip the pasta and broccoli into a bowl and leave to cool. After cooled, add the pine nuts, vinegar, pesto and tomatoes and toss thoroughly.

BEAUTIFUL BEET & WALNUT COUSCOUS SALAD

Ingredients

- 180g of pre-cooked couscous
- 50g of walnuts
- 50g of crumbled goat's cheese
- 4 diced cooked beetroot
- Zest and juice of 1 orange
- 75g of baby spinach leaves
- 20g of watercress
- Juice of half an lemon
- 2 tbsp of olive oil

How to make:

- Add all the ingredients to a bowl and toss thoroughly, serve immediately.

ALMOND, CRANBERRY & SPINACH SALAD

Ingredients

- 100g of Almonds
- 75g of baby spinach
- 75g of rocket
- 1 cup of dried cranberries
- 1 tbsp of poppy seeds
- 20g of white sugar
- 3 tbsp of minced onion
- 2 tbsp of white wine vinegar
- 2 tbsp of cider vinegar
- 2 tbsp of vegetable oil
- 2 tbsp of toasted sesame seeds

How to make

- In a bowl, add the poppy seeds, sugar, sesame seeds, onion, white vinegar, cider vinegar and vegetable oil and whisk together. Add the spinach, almonds and cranberries and toss.

APPLE, ALMOND, FETA & SPINACH SALAD

Ingredients

- 100g of spinach, rocket and watercress mix
- 2 cored and chopped apples
- 50g of almonds
- 1 diced red onion
- 75g of crumbled feta cheese
- 3 tbsp of red wine vinegar

How to make:

- Mix all the ingredients together in a large salad bowl and toss thoroughly. Serve immediately.

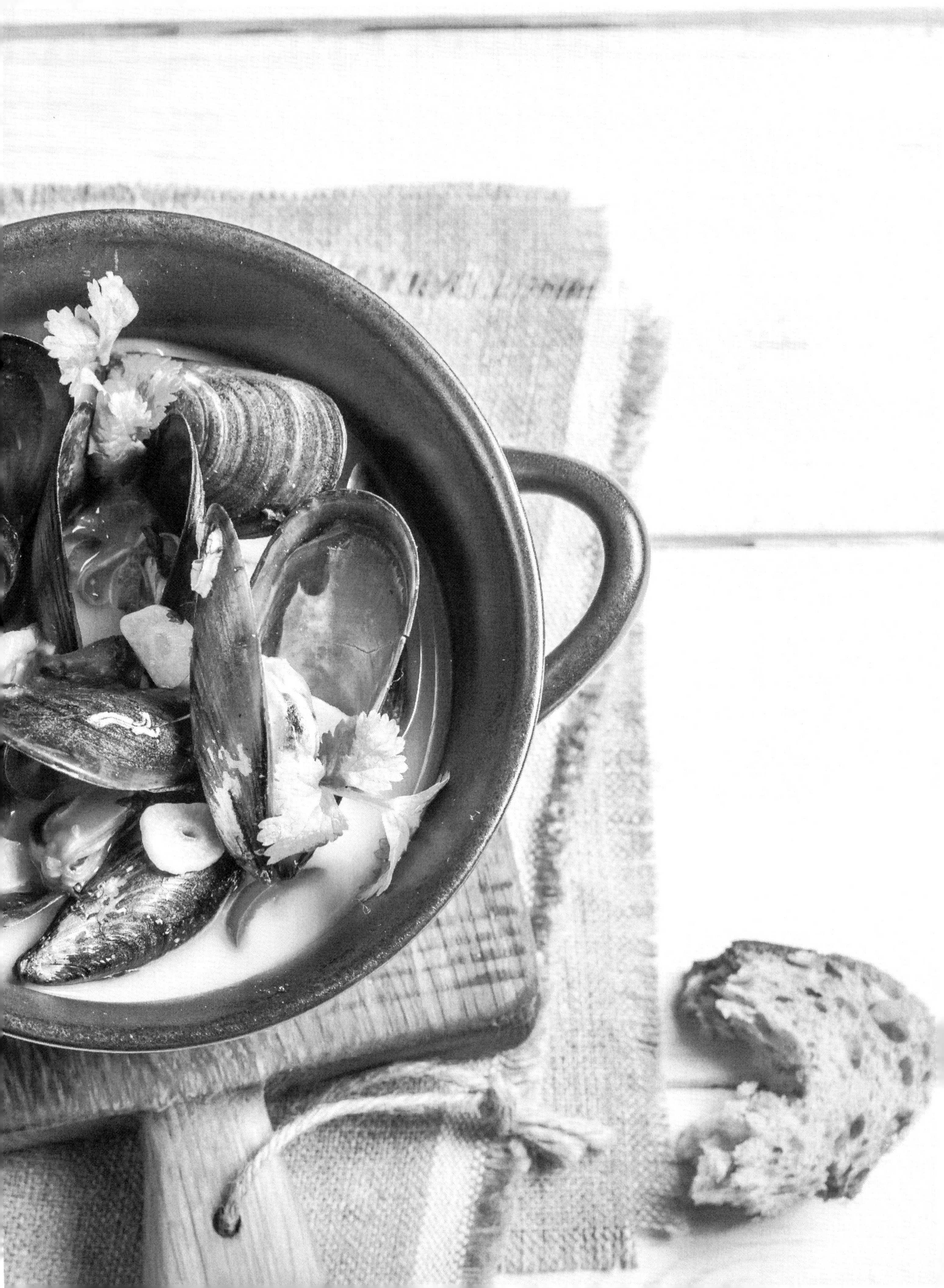

SEAFOOD AND FISH SALADS

Seafood is delicious and always best enjoyed with complimentary sides. A seafood salad is the perfect way to enjoy a taste of the ocean. Just think about the delightful goodness – all the omega 3, vitamins and nutrients packed into the recipes!

DIVINE CRAB & ROCKET SALAD

Ingredients

- 400g of crabmeat
- 100g of rocket leaves
- 3 tbsp of olive oil
- 100ml of crème fraiche
- 1 diced, peeled and stoned avocado
- 14 halved cherry tomatoes
- Juice of 1 lemon

How to make:

- Get a small bowl and add the crabmeat. Add the lemon juice and crème fraiche and stir until smooth. Add some salt and pepper and leave to one side.
- In a salad bowl, add the rocket, tomatoes and avocado. Drizzle with the olive oil, add some salt and pepper and then toss thoroughly. Evenly add the crabmeat to the salad, drizzle the lemony crème fraiche over the salad and serve.

LEMONY PRAWN & CHORIZO SALAD

Ingredients

- 120g of baby spinach
- Handful of chopped parsley
- 100g of raw king prawns
- 120g of chopped chorizo
- 1 finely sliced red onion
- 350g of drained and rinsed chickpeas
- 3 diced aubergines
- 6 tbsp of olive oil
- 1 crushed garlic clove
- Zest and juice of 1 lemon
- 1 tsp of ground cumin
- 2 tsp of clear honey

How to make:

- Heat oil in a large griddle pan over a medium heat. Sprinkle some salt and pepper over the aubergine and place in pan. Fry until slightly charred. Remove and place to one side.
- Meanwhile get a bowl and mix the olive oil, lemon juice, zest, cumin, honey, garlic and salt together to form the dressing.
- Add the prawns to the griddle pan and fry for 2 minutess, turning them over halfway through, then place to one side.
- Add the chorizo to the pan and fry for 8 minutes, turning them over halfway through.
- Get a large salad bowl and add the baby spinach, chickpeas, parley and red onions. Then add the prawns, chorizo and aubergines and toss through. Finish off the salad by drizzling the dressing all over the top.
- Enjoy.

BEANY TUNA SALAD

Ingredients:

- 200g of drained tuna
- 1 tbsp of olive oil
- 300g of drained and rinsed cannellini beans
- 1 tsp of Dijon mustard
- Zest and juice of 1 lemon
- Handful of chopped dill
- Handful of chopped parsley
- 1 diced fennel bulb
- 1 chopped cucumber
- 2 tbsp of pumpkin seeds
- 1 tsp of chilli flakes

How to make:

- In a bowl, add the chilli, mustard, oil, zest, juice and some good old salt and pepper. Mix them together.
- Get a large salad bowl and add the rest of the ingredients and toss thoroughly
- Finish by drizzling the dressing over the salad.

FLAKED HADDOCK & WATERCRESS SALAD

Ingredients

- 100g of flaked smoked haddock
- 100g of cooked couscous
- Juice of 1 orange
- Large handful of watercress
- 90g of steamed, diced thin-stemmed broccoli

How to make:

Mix all the ingredients together in large salad bowl and toss thoroughly.

SWEET HONEY SALMON SALAD

Ingredients:

- Handful of rocket
- Handful of lamb's lettuce
- Handful of baby spinach leaves
- 1 chopped, peeled and stoned avocado
- 3 cooked, flaked salmon fillets
- Handful of chopped coriander
- 80g of sugar snap peas
- 1 tbsp of soy sauce
- 3 tsp of vinegar
- 1 tsp of clear honey
- 1 tbsp of sherry
- 1tbsp of boiling hot water

How to make

- Mix the honey, soy sauce, vinegar, boiling hot water and sherry together and whisk well.
- Add all the salad ingredients to a bowl and toss thoroughly. Serve with the dressing on top.

SCALLOPS, WATERCRESS AND SHALLOT SALAD

Ingredients

- 8 scallops
- 2 large chopped garlic cloves
- 1 tsp chopped fresh red chilli
- 1 finely chopped shallot
- 100g of watercress
- 1 tsp of chopped parsley
- 2 tbsp of olive oil

How to make:

- Add the scallops to a bowl with the olive oil, lemon juice, shallot and black pepper. Mix everything together and leave for around 5 minutes to soak.
- Add the scallops mix to medium heated pan and fry for 1 minute until they are golden. Then turn them over and cook for 1 minute more.
- Remove and place to one side.
- Get a salad bowl and add the watercress, parley, garlic and chill. Place the scallops on top and serve ASAP!

TUNA & BLACK OLIVE SPINACH SALAD

Ingredients

- 2 Cans of tinned tuna in olive oil
- Handful of baby spinach
- 1 Chopped red onion
- 300g of chopped peppers
- 1 tbsp Olive oil
- 1 Chopped red chilli
- 350g of halved cherry tomatoes
- 1 Cup of chopped black olives
- Salt
- Pepper

How to make:

- Heat oil in a pan and fry the onions, peppers and chilli.
- Get a bowl and add onion mix, tomatoes, tuna, baby spinach and olives and toss thoroughly. Season with some salt and pepper.

RED PEPPER SQUID & CHICKPEA SALAD

Ingredients

- 350g of squid (chopped into rings)
- 3 red peppers
- 1 diced chilli
- 80ml of olive oil
- 600g of rinsed and drained chickpeas
- 2 finely chopped garlic cloves
- Juice and zest from 1 lemon

How to make:

- Get a griddle pan a pre-heat to a high heat. Place the peppers in the pan and cook until charred. Remove the peppers, deseed and thinly slice.
- In a bowl mix the chickpeas, chilli, garlic, juices and peppers and place to one side.
- Pre-heat a large pan until it's steaming. Add some oil to the pan and stir fry the squid for around 1 – 2 minutes. Remove the squid from the pan and add to the bowl with the chickpeas. Drizzle with the remaining oil, lemon and lemon zest. Serve.

DIVINE EGG & FLAKED SALMON CAESAR SALAD

Ingredients

- 4 quartered boiled eggs
- 125g of smoked salmon flakes
- 2 tsp of capers
- 75g of ready-made croutons
- 5 tbsp of Caesar dressing
- 2 little gem lettuces
- Handful of watercress

How to make:

- Add the leaves from the lettuce, capers, watercress, croutons, eggs and salmon to a large salad bowl. Finish by drizzling the salad with the Caesar dressing.

BLACK OLIVE & SARDINE SALAD

Ingredients

- 240g of canned sardines
- 1 tbsp of drained caper
- Handful of chopped black olives
- 2 tbsp of olive oil
- 2 tbsp of red wine vinegar
- 100g bag of mixed salad leaves
- Salt
- Pepper

How to make:

- Mix all the ingredients together in large salad bowl and toss thoroughly.

SPICY TUNA & BLACK BEAN SALAD

Ingredients

- 400g of drained, canned and flaked tuna
- 8 halved cherry tomatoes
- 1 chopped red chilli
- Handful of chopped spring onions
- 1 chopped avocado
- 200g of drained and rinsed black beans
- 200g of drained and rinsed cannellini beans
- 3 tbsp of French dressing

-

How to make:

- In a bowl, mix the beans, tomatoes, onions, chilli and avocado together. Add the tuna to the salad along with the salad dressing. Toss gently and serve.

PRAWN & HERB NOODLE SALAD

Ingredients

- 350g of pre-cooked, peeled king prawns
- 75g of dried rice noodles
- 1 diced cucumber
- Handful of chopped coriander leaves
- Handful of chopped mint leaves
- 1 tbsp of olive oil
- 1 crushed garlic clove
- Zest and juice of 1 lemon or lime
- Handful of lettuce leaves

How to make:

- Add the rice noodle to some boiling hot water and leave for around 5 – 6 minutes. Drain and rinse.
- Place the rice noodles in a bowl with the diced cucumber and the king prawns.
- Mix the olive oil, coriander, mint, zest and juice, lettuce and garlic clove together. Add the mix to the bowl with the noodles and toss.

SMOKY SALMON AND ROCKET RICE SALAD

Ingredients

- 300g of cooked brown rice
- Handful of rocket leaves
- Handful of watercress leaves
- 80g of cooked, diced oak smoked salmon
- 1 diced cucumber
- Handful of chopped spring onion
- 2 tbsp of rice vinegar
- 2 tbsp of sesame oil
- zest and juice of 1 lemon
- ½ tsp of sugar

How to make:

- In a small bowl, whisk the rice vinegar, sesame oil, lemon and sugar. Get a large salad bowl; add the rest of the ingredients and toss. Drizzle the dressing over the top and serve

SHRIMP, AVOCADO & CHERRY TOMATO SALAD

Ingredients

- 400g of cooked, deveined and diced shrimp
- 2 peeled, cored and chopped avocados
- 10 halved cherry tomato's
- 1 chopped onion
- 1 large diced green pepper
- 2 tbsp of lime juice
- Handful of baby spinach
- Small handful of chopped cilantro
- Salt
- Pepper

How to Make

- Add the shrimp, avocado, onion, tomatoes, peppers, baby spinach, cilantro and lime juice to a large salad bowl. Sprinkle some salt and pepper over the top, toss and serve.

LOBSTER SALAD

Ingredients

- 200g of shredded, cooked lobster
- 4 diced bell peppers
- 6 diced celery stalks
- 1 diced red onion
- 3 tbsp of low-fat mayonnaise
- 1 tbsp of black pepper
- 50g of rocket

How to make:

- Get a large salad bowl and mix the lobster meat, peppers, celery, onion, mayonnaise, rocket and black pepper together. Serve chilled.

QUINOA, SPINACH & TUNA SALAD

Ingredients

- 100g of pre-cooked quinoa
- Handful of chopped olives
- 200g of drained, canned tuna
- Handful of chopped spinach
- 3 tbsp of olive oil
- 2 tbsp of chopped fresh cilantro
- 1 can of drained and rinsed black beans

How to make:

- Add all the ingredients to a large bowl and toss thoroughly. Leave in the fridge for two hours and serve..

DELICIOUS TUNA SALAD NICOISE

Ingredients

- 200g of canned, tinned tuna
- 4 quarter boiled eggs
- 100g of diced, boiled new potatoes
- 4 diced tomatoes
- 4 anchovy filets
- 3 tbsp of lemon vinaigrette
- Handful of chopped, pitted nicoise olives
- Handful of chopped parsley
- 100g bag of mixed salad

How to make:

- In a large bowl and the potatoes, onion, olives, parsley, eggs, capers, anchovies and tomatoes. Drizzle over the vinaigrette and toss.

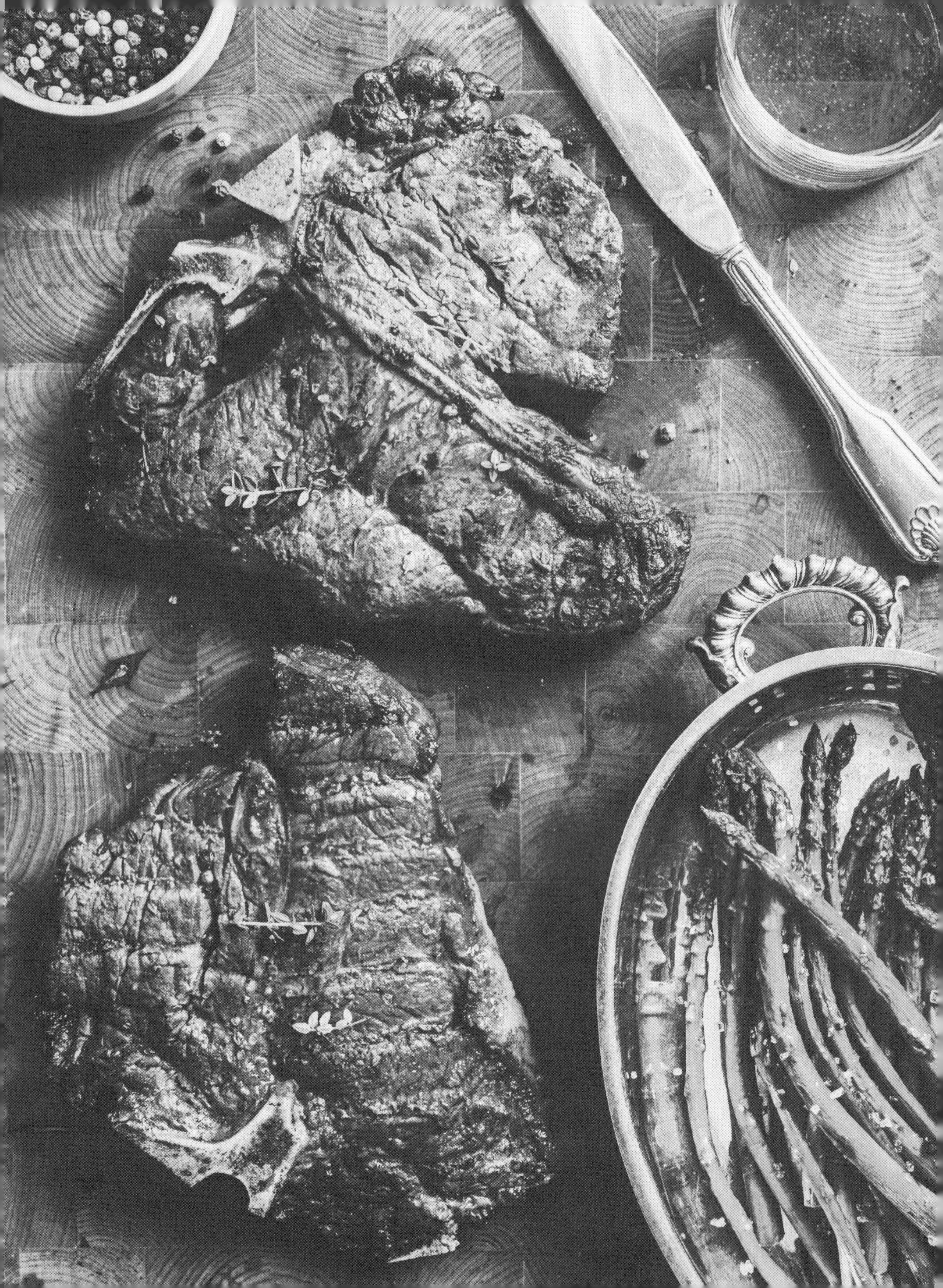

MEATY SALADS

So, if you haven't already managed to convert the masses to your lovely salads, these will be the recipes that help! There is certainly a place for all meats in salads and the possibilities are endless. Different meats are great teamed with fruit and herbs so use my suggestions to experiment with your meaty mouthfuls.

GORGEOUS SMOKED BACON, EGGS, ASPARAGUS & WALNUTS

Ingredients

- 8 rashers of smoked bacon
- 4 boiled, quartered eggs
- 25 of cooked asparagus spears
- Handful of watercress
- 50g of walnuts
- 2 tsp smooth French mustard
- 1 tbsp of cider vinegar
- 2 tbsp of rapeseed oil
- 3 tbsp of hazelnut oil

How to make:

- Heat a griddle pan to a high heat and cook the bacon for around 5-6 minutes until crispy. To make the dressing, add the cider vinegar, rapeseed oil, hazelnut and the French mustard to a bowl and whisk together.
- Add the watercress, asparagus, walnuts, eggs and bacon to a bowl and toss. Finish of the dish by drizzling the dressing over the top.

PEPPER CHICKEN & HAM SALAD

Ingredients

- 4 cooked, diced chicken breasts
- 100g of diced ham
- 50g of lamb's lettuce
- 50g of oak leaf
- Sprinkle of salt
- Sprinkle of pepper
- 50g of baby spinach
- 4 roasted, diced red peppers
- Juice and zest of 1 lemon
- 1 crushed garlic clove
- 120g of low-fat natural yogurt

How to make:

- Get a bowl and whisk the lemon, zest, garlic, salt, pepper and yogurt together until smooth. Add the leaves, chicken, ham, peppers and the dressing into a large salad bowl and toss well

OLLIE'S BBQ CHICKEN & PINEAPPLE SALAD

Ingredients

- 150g of pre-cooked BBQ chicken
- 25g of baby spinach
- 25g of watercress
- 25g of rocket
- 25g of lamb's lettuce
- 1 diced grilled red pepper
- 200g of canned pineapples
- Small handful of coriander
- Small handful of cherry tomatoes
- 1 chopped red chilli
- 2 tbsp of sweet chilli sauce
- 3 tbsp of white wine vinegar

How to make:

- Firstly, mix 3 tbsp of the pineapple juice from the can, with the red chilli, sweet chilli sauce and white wine vinegar in a small bowl.
- Add the other ingredients into a large salad bowl and toss with the dressing.

SUPER CAESAR SALAD

Ingredients

- 4 diced, cooked chicken thigh meat (with skin)
- 40g of grated parmesan
- 50g of whole-wheat croutons
- 2 tbsp of Worchester sauce
- 1 crushed garlic clove
- 4 diced little gem lettuces
- Handful of chopped spring onions
- Handful of rocket
- 100 ml of low fat mayonnaise
- Salt
- Pepper

How to make:

- In a large salad bowl mix all the ingredients together and finish of by sprinkle some extra Parmesan over the top. Remember to toss well.

HORSY HAM SALAD

Ingredients

- 100g of ham
- 300g of boiled new baby potatoes
- 3 tbsp of Greek yogurt
- 3 tsp of horseradish
- 120g of mixed salad
- 2 quartered boiled eggs
- Salt
- Pepper

How to make:

- Mix the yogurt, horseradish and 2 tbsp of water together to make the dressing. Mix the other ingredients in a large salad bowl. Add the dressing, toss and serve.

TUNA TURKEY SALAD

Ingredients

- 300g of diced, cooked turkey meat
- 2 chopped tomatoes
- 50g of rocket
- 50g of watercress
- 1 tbsp of drained capers
- 2 tbsp of olive oil
- 80g of low-fat mayonnaise
- 1 diced anchovy
- 100g of canned tuna
- Juice of 1 lemon

How to make:

- Get a food process and add the mayo, anchovy, lemon juice, tuna and capers an mix until everything is fully mixed together. Get a large salad bowl and add the rocket, watercress, chopped tomatoes and turkey. Add the dressing and serve right away.

FETA, LENTILS, CHICKEN & PEACH SALAD

Ingredients

- 100g of cooked lentils
- 400g of pre-cooked chicken breasts
- 80g of crumbled feta chesse
- 2 diced peaches
- 25g of chopped mint
- 25g of chopped dill
- Juice and zest of 2 limes
- 1 tsp of white wine vinegar
- 2 tbsp of olive oil
- 1 tbsp of wholegrain mustard
- 1 crushed garlic clove

How to make:

- Firstly, mix the white wine, olive oil, mustard, garlic and juice and zest together to make the dressing. Get a bowl and add all the other ingredients. Drizzle the dressing over the top, toss, then serve.

ROCKET & CASHEW NUT SALAD WITH POACHED BEEF

Ingredients

- 450g of beef fillet joint
- 1 chopped carrot
- 1 diced red onion
- 1l of stock
- 3 springs of rosemary
- 4 bay leaves
- 50g of baby spinach
- 50g of rocket
- 3 tbsp of olive oil
- 1 tbsp of balsamic vinegar
- 1 tsp of Dijon mustard
- 50g of chopped cashew nuts

How to make:

- Boil the stock with the herbs, carrots and onion. Once it comes to the boil, cover and let simmer for around 8 – 10 minutes. Meanwhile cut any sinew off the beef joint. Add some salt and pepper to the beef and place in the stock. Cover than gently simmer for around 18 – 24 minutes dependant on how you like your beef. When done, remove the beef from the pan and leave the beef to cool. Dice the beef up.
- In a small bowl, mix the olive oil, mustard, vinegar & 2 tbsp of the stock together to make the dressing.
- In a large salad bowl add all of the other ingredients together and toss with the dressing

DIVINE STEAK AND RED WINE SALAD

Ingredients

- 220g of frying steak
- 2 tbsp of Olive oil
- 1 tsp of crusted celery seeds
- 10 halved cherry tomatoes
- Small handful of watercress
- 4 chopped tomatoes
- 2 tbsp of Worcestershire sauce
- 1 tbsp of horseradish sauce
- 1 tsp of red wine vinegar
- 1 tsp of tomato puree
- 8 thinly sliced celery sticks

How to make:

- Get the frying steak and brush with a tsp of olive oil, and then rub both sides with some salt, pepper, celery seeds and 1 tbsp of Worcester sauce.
- In a small bowl add a tbsp of horseradish sauce, red wine vinegar, tomato puree and horseradish sauce to make the dressing
- Pre heat a griddle pan to a high heat and the fry the steaks for around 4 – 6 minutes, turning them over half way through. Remove the steak from the pan and place to one side.
- In a large salad bowl, add all the other ingredients and when ready, dice the steak up, add to the top and drizzle with the dressing.

BEAN AND BARLEY CHICKEN SALAD

Ingredients

- 1 small cooked chicken
- 100g pearl barley
- 100g green beans, trimmed
- 1 small red onion, sliced thinly
- 10 cherry tomatoes, halved
- 50g toasted pine nuts
- Handful of finely chopped fresh basil.
- Juice of 1 lemon
- 3 tbsp red wine vinegar
- 5 tbsp olive oil

How to make:

- Shred the chicken meat from the bones and set aside.
- Cook the pearl barley by boiling in salted water for approx. 20 minutes. Whilst boiling, steam the green beans for the last 10 minutes using a colander over the pan.
- Drain barley and beans and combine in a large bowl.
- Add the red onion, tomatoes, pine nuts and basil.
- Serve with the whisked dressing ingredients.

WHOLESOME CHICKEN AND CORN ON THE COB SALAD

Ingredients

- 2 chicken breasts, legs or thighs (skin on)
- 2 garlic cloves, finely chopped
- 1 tbsp paprika
- Juice of 2 lemon
- 2 tbsp olive oil
- 2 corn on the cobs
- ½ washed and sliced cos lettuce
- ½ diced cucumber

How to make:

- Whisk together the garlic, paprika, ½ lemon juice and 1 tbsp oil with salt and pepper – marinate the chicken for as long as possible.
- Preheat the grill to a medium-high heat and grill the chicken for at least 10 minutes on each side or until the juices run clear.
- Drizzle the remaining oil over the corn on the cob and grill each side for at least 3-4 minutes.
- Slice the corn from the cob with a sharp knife.
- Serve the chicken (sliced if breasts or whole if thigh/legs) with the corn, cucumber and the lettuce. Squeeze over the remaining lemon juice and season with salt and pepper to taste.

PERFECT BACON, LETTUCE & TOMATO SALAD

Ingredients

- 400g of bacon
- 1 head of diced lamb lettuce
- 2 chopped beef tomatoes
- Handful of lamb lettuce
- 50g of whole-wheat croutons
- Salt
- Pepper
- 1 crushed garlic
- 4 tbsp of low-fat mayonnaise
- ½ juice of 1 lemon

How to make:

- Get a deep skillet and heat to a high heat. Add the bacon and cook until evenly browned on both sides. Crumble the bacon and set to one side.
- In a food processor, add the mayonnaise, garlic, pepper, salt and juice and whizz until smooth. Get a large salad bowl and add the tomatoes, bacon, croutons and lamb lettuce. Mix with the dressing and serve.

BACON, WALNUT AND CRUMBLED GORGONZOLA SALAD

Ingredients

- 4 slices of cooked, crumbled streaky turkey bacon
- 50g of crumbled gorgonzola cheese
- 100g bag of mixed salad
- Handful of walnuts
- 1 minced garlic cloves
- Salt
- Pepper
- 3 tbsp of olive oil
- 2 tbsp of red wine vinegar

How to make:

- In a food processor, mix the olive oil vinegar, salt, pepper, garlic and cheese to make the dressing.
- In a large salad bowl, add all the other ingredients and toss with the dressing.

CHORIZO, YAM & EGG SALAD

Ingredients

- 4 quartered boiled eggs
- 2 large cooked yams
- 85g of diced cooked chorizo
- 1 crushed garlic clove
- Juice of 1 lemon
- 3 tbsp of olive oil
- 80g of halved cherry tomatoes
- 100g of mixed salad leaves

How to make:

- Mix all the ingredients in a salad bowl and toss thoroughly.

TURKEY HAM & SWEET SYRUP SALAD

Ingredients

- 100g of shredded turkey ham
- 2 tbsp of olive oil
- 1 tbsp of red wine vinegar
- 2 tbp of maple syrup
- Handful of shredded cabbage
- Handful of baby spinach
- 1 tsp of wholegrain mustard
- 4 ready to eat dried apricots
- 1 chopped shallot
- Handful of walnut pieces
- 2 tbsp of chopped parsley

How to make:

- Mix the mustard, vinegar, oil and maple syrup together. Add the cabbage, shots, walnuts and apricots. Toss with the shredded turkey ham.

HIPSTER MOROCCAN CHICKEN SALAD

Ingredients

- 500g of cooked, shredded chicken breast
- 2 chopped aubergine
- 2 tbsp of olive oil
- 100g of watercress
- 100g of pomegranate seeds
- 20 halved cherry tomatoes
- 1 tbsp of harissa

How to make:

- Mix all the ingredients together in a large salad bowl. Goes really well with whole-wheat pitta bread.

DELICIOUS DUCK & RICE NOODLE SALAD

Ingredients

- 1 duck leg
- 100g of rice noodles
- 3 chopped spring onions
- 2 tbsp of hoisin sauce
- 1 tbsp of soy sauce
- 1 diced celery stick
- 1 diced carrot
- Half a diced cucumber
- 2 tbsp of chinese five-spice powder

How to make:

- Pre-heat an oven to 220c/gas 7. Season the duck leg on both sides with the five-spice, place on a tray and cook for 25-30 minutes.
- While the duck is cooking, cook the noodles using the packet instructions, then drain and let cool.
- In a small bowl, mix the soy, hoisin with a tbsp of water. Mix the celery, cucumber, onions and carrots in a large bowl along with the noodles. Cut the meat of the bone and add to the bowl. Finish of the salad by drizzling over the dressing.

DUCK EGG, SUNDRIED TOMATOES, MUSHROOM & SHREDDED HAM SALAD

Ingredients

- 2 boiled, quartered duck eggs
- 100g of shredded ham
- 20 halved cherry tomatoes
- 100g of mixed salad leaves
- 50g of sundried tomatoes and oil
- 1 crushed garlic clove
- Handful of cooked, sliced mushrooms
- 1 tbsp of olive oil
- 50g of croutons

How to make:

- Mix the ham with the cherry tomatoes, mushrooms, sun-dried tomatoes and oils together and toss. Top with the duck eggs and croutons.

BULGUR WHEAT, CARROT & HAM SALAD

Ingredients

- 200g of shredded ham
- 200g of pre-cooked bulgur wheat
- 2 finely sliced carrots
- 5 finely chopped celery sticks
- Handful of chopped parsley
- 2 tbsp of olive oil
- 2 tbsp of red wine vinegar
- 1 tbsp of wholegrain mustard
- Handful of baby spinach
- Handful of rocket

How to make:

- Firstly, mix the olive oil, vinegar and mustard together to form the dressing. In a large salad bowl, mix all the other ingredients together and drizzle with the dressing.

CHORIZO, SUNDRIED TOMATO & CHILI SALAD

Ingredients

- 120g of diced chorizo
- 4 diced beef tomatoes
- Handful of sundried tomatoes
- 1 diced onion
- 1 tbsp of red wine vinegar
- 2 tbsp of olive oil
- 1 diced red chilli

How to make:

- Pre heat a pan and fry the chorizo until it's browned on both sides. Add all the ingredients to a salad bowl and toss thoroughly to let the vinegar and oil soak through.

GOURMET BROCCOLI & BACON SALAD

Ingredients

- 4 cooked, crumble bacon rashers
- 2 heads of chopped, boiled broccoli
- 50g of crumbled goat's cheese
- 2 tbsp of red wine vinegar
- Salt
- Pepper
- Juice of 1 lemon
- 3 tbsp of low-fat mayonnaise

How to make:

- Make the dressing by mixing the vinegar, pepper, salt, mayonnaise and lemon juice. In a large bowl toss all of the other ingredients with the dressing and serve.

PORKY PEAR AND HAZELNUT SALAD

Ingredients

- 500g of cooked, diced pork steak
- 1 tbsp of olive oil
- 1 tbsp of chopped parsley
- 50g of baby spinach
- 50g of rocket
- 1 cored and sliced pear
- 50g of hazelnuts
- 2 tbsp of balsamic vinegar

How to make:

- Mix all the ingredients together in a large boss and drizzle the vinegar over the top to serve.

SAUCY STEAK AND CRANBERRY SALAD

Ingredients

- 500g sliced, pre-cooked steak
- 50g of dried cranberries
- 1 sliced beef tomato
- Salt
- Pepper
- 50g of walnuts
- 50g of rocket
- 50g of baby spinach
- 50g of watercress
- 2 tbsp of olive oil

How to make

- Pre-heat a griddle pan to a high heat. Cook the steak for around 4-6 minutes turning half way through. Get a bowl and add all the salad ingredients along with the steak and toss. Drizzle some olive oil over the top and serve.

AWESOME BEEF NACHO SALAD

Ingredients

- 1 pound lean ground beef
- 1 tspn paprika
- a pinch of salt and black pepper
- 1 tspn chilli powder
- 1/2 (14.5 ounce) tortilla chips
- 1 packet of grated mozzarella
- 1/2 (15 ounce) can kidney beans, drained
- Handful chopped iceberg lettuce
- 1 chopped white onion
- 1 chopped avocado
- 2 sliced beef tomatoes

How to make:

- Fry beef in a large pan on a medium-high heat, stirring until browned.
- Throw in the onions and kidney beans and stir in with the beef to cook for 20-30 minutes. Sprinkle over the spices and seasoning.
- Place the chips into a bowl and then pour over the beef and onions.
- Layer with the tomatoes and avocado, cheese and lettuce.

TENDER-STEM BROCCOLI, PANCETTA AND PINE NUT SALAD

Ingredients

- 1 packet of tender-stem broccoli
- 1 cup raisins
- 1/2 chopped red onion
- ½ cup pine nuts
- 1 tbsp olive oil
- drizzle of balsamic vinegar

How to make:

- Boil a saucepan of seasoned water and steam the broccoli over the pan in a colander. Meanwhile, place cubed pancetta in a pan and cook over medium-high heat for 10 minutes. Keep turning until browned. Remove from pan and allow to cool (use kitchen towel to soak up excess fat). Remove the broccoli and set aside.
- Now mix the pancetta, broccoli, raisins, and onion together in a large bowl. Stir the olive oil and balsamic vinegar in a separate dish and pour over your salad when ready to serve. Toss through for an even coating and season with salt and pepper to taste.

ASIAN INSPIRED GINGER BEEF AND SUGAR SNAP PEA INFUSION

Ingredients

- 3/4 pound rump or sirloin steak, cut into thin slices
- 1 tablespoon canola oil
- 2 cloves garlic, finely chopped
- 1 teaspoon grated fresh ginger
- A pinch of salt and black pepper
- 1/4 cup soy sauce
- 1/4 cup rice vinegar
- 1 (thumb-size) piece peeled fresh ginger -grated
- 2 tablespoons chopped fresh cilantro
- 1 tablespoon sesame oil
- 2 teaspoons chilli paste
- 1 clove garlic, minced
- 1 pack of sugar snap peas
- 1/2 chopped white onion
- 1 small cucumber, cut into ribbons
- 1/4 cup chopped peanuts
- Chopped fresh cilantro
- Fresh lime wedges

How to make:

- Marinade the beef with the oil, garlic and ginger with salt and pepper sprinkled to taste. Leave in its bowl for as long as possible (preferably overnight).
- Heat a non-stick pan over a very high heat; once smoking fry the beef (you don't need to use extra oil for this).
- Turn the beef after a few minutes and brown on each side until cooked to taste (rare-well done). You will be able to tell as the side of each beef slice turns from pink to brown from the edges to the middle. allow a little pink in the middle if you don't like your steak too well done!
- Take off the heat and place to one side.
- Stir in the sugar snap peas (raw or steamed), onion and cucumber in with the beef. large bowl.
- Add the salad dressing just before serving.
- Add the peanuts, fresh lime wedges and cilantro to top the salad.
- Beat all of the salad dressing ingredients into a separate bowl.

LAMB, WATERCRESS AND MINT SALAD

Ingredients

- 1 bag of baby watercress
- 1-2 cooked lamb breasts
- 1 sprig of chopped fresh mint
- 10 cherry tomatoes
- 1 tbsp olive oil

How to make:

- Stir the mint into the olive oil and add salt and pepper. Slice the lamb breasts and add to the watercress. Throw in the halved cherry tomatoes. Dress with the olive oil and mint.

SPICY PARADISE SALAD

Ingredients

- 2 skinless, boneless chicken breasts
- 1/2 cup teriyaki marinade
- 2 beef tomatoes, seeded and chopped
- 1/2 chopped white onion
- 2 finely chopped jalapenos
- 2 teaspoons chopped fresh cilantro
- 1 tbsp Dijon mustard
- 1 tbsp honey
- 1 1/2 tablespoons white sugar
- 1 tablespoon vegetable oil
- 1 1/2 tablespoons cider vinegar
- 1 1/2 teaspoons lime juice
- 1 bag of mixed salad leaves.
- 1 (8 ounce) can pineapple chunks, drained

How to make:

- Marinate the chicken in the teriyaki sauce for at least 1 hour up to 1 night.
- Separately mix the tomatoes, onion and jalapenos to make a salsa. Cover and refrigerate.
- In another bowl mix the oils, vinegars and lime juice. Cover and refrigerate.
- Preheat the grill at a high heat.
- Grill the chicken breasts for 14-16 minutes, turning half way through. Make sure the juices run clear before serving.
- Serve the mixed salad greens with a dollop of salsa and sprinkled pineapple chunks. Slice and serve the chicken breasts over each salad and dress the salad with the pre-prepared dressing to serve.

CHICKEN BACON AND AVOCADO SALAD

Ingredients

- 2 boneless cooked and diced chicken breasts.
- 2 tbsp mayonnaise
- 1 avocado peeled and diced.
- Cooked and diced bacon
- Lamb's lettuce, washed and sliced.

How to make:

- Combine all ingredients in a large salad bowl. Add mayonnaise, salt and pepper, and stir.

CHICKEN AND ANCHOVY SALAD

Ingredients

- Strips of cooked chicken breast.
- Croutons (either pre-bought or homemade by cutting bread into cubes and lightly frying in a pan until toasted).
- 1 tablespoon light olive oil
- 1 head romaine lettuce- rinsed, dried and sliced
- 2 small garlic cloves, finely chopped
- 1 -2 anchovies finely sliced.
- The juice from 1 lemon
- 1 teaspoon Dijon mustard
- 1 teaspoon Worcestershire sauce
- 1 cup mayonnaise
- 1/2 cup freshly grated parmesan
- a pinch of salt and pepper.

How to make:

- Whisk the garlic, anchovies, lemon juice, mustard and Worcestershire sauce before adding the parmesan and salt and pepper and continuing to whisk until smooth. Add the romaine lettuce, chicken, croutons in a bowl. Pour over the homemade dressing and season to taste. Add freshly shaved parmesan to serve.

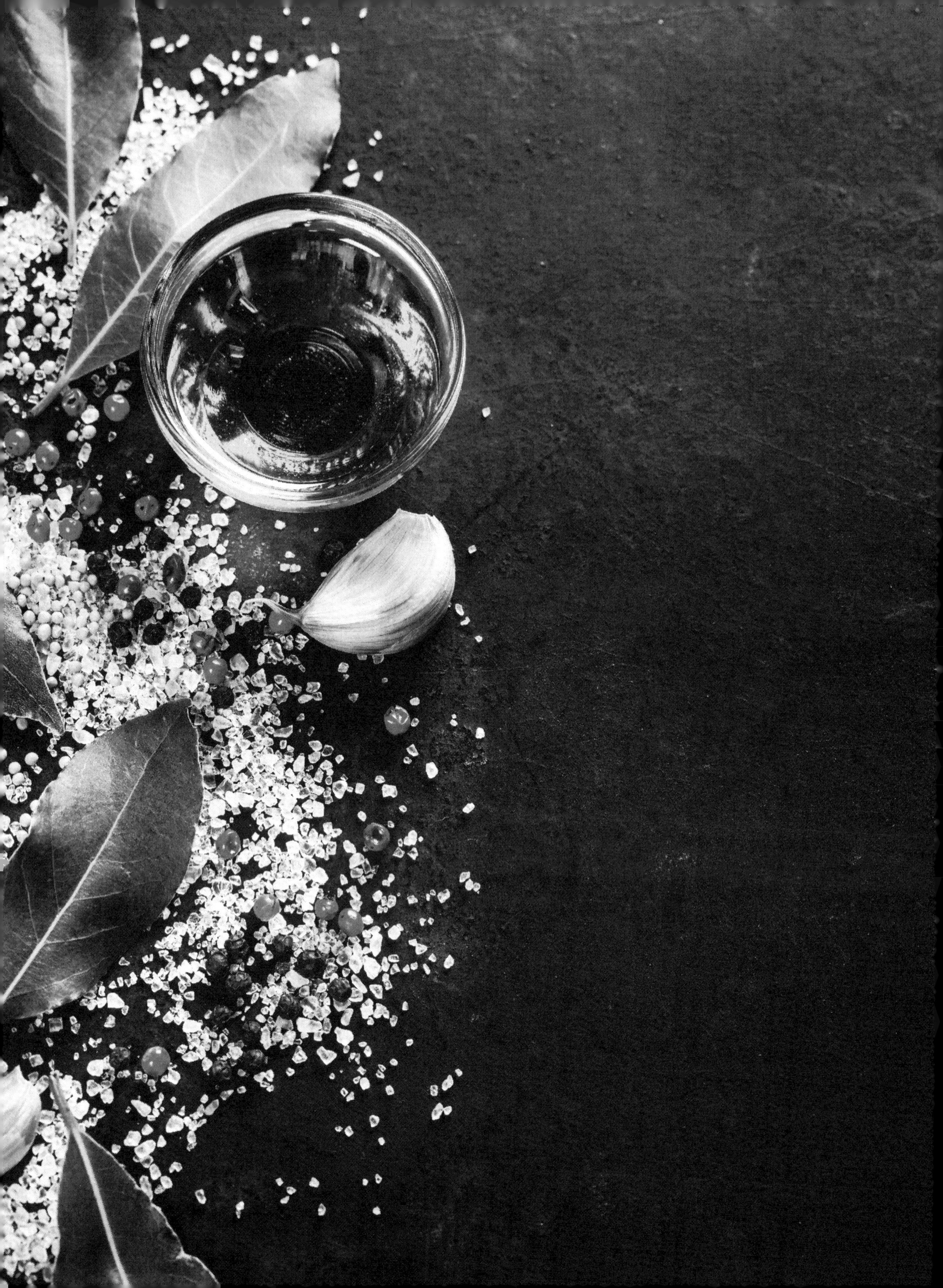

DRESSINGS

As previously mentioned, homemade dressings are the perfect accompaniment to your salads. Here are my favourite recipes to make the staple dressings, perfect for all of your salads.

HIPSTER VINAIGRETTE

Ingredients

- 2 tbsp of Dijon mustard
- 2 tbsp of red wine vinegar
- Salt
- Pepper
- 1 tbsp of olive oil

How to make:

Whisk all the ingredients together in a small bowl.

WHITE WINE VINAIGRETTE

Ingredients

- 2 tbsp of Dijon mustard
- 2 tbsp of white wine vinegar
- Salt
- Pepper
- 1 tbsp of olive oil

How to make:

Whisk all the ingredients together in a small bowl or food processer.

SWEET MUSTARD VINAIGRETTE

Ingredients

- 2 tbsp of Dijon mustard
- 2 tbsp of honey
- 1 tbsp of lime juice
- 2 tbsp of of chopped tyme
- 2 tbsp of white wine vinegar
- Salt
- Pepper
- 1 tbsp of olive oil
- 1tbsp of minced jalapeno

How to make:

Whisk all the ingredients together in a food processer.

BEAUTIFUL BACON

Ingredients

- 2 tbsp of Dijon mustard
- 2 tbsp of red wine vinegar
- Salt
- Pepper
- 1 tbsp of olive oil
- 20g of crumbled blue chesse
- 2 crumbed cooked bacon rashers
- 1 tbsp of chopped chives

How to make:

Whisk all the ingredients together in a food processer.

ITALIAN SURPRISE

Ingredients

- 2 tbsp of Dijon mustard
- 2 tbsp of red wine vinegar
- Salt
- Pepper
- 1 tbsp of olive oil
- 20g of crumbled feta
- 4 diced cherry tomatoes
- 1 tbsp of chopped parsley
- 1 tsp of fried oregano

How to make:

Whisk all the ingredients together in a food processer.

POSH TRUFFLE DRESSING

Ingredients

- 1 tbsp Dijon mustard
- 1 tbsp champagne (or white wine) vinegar
- 1 finely chopped shallot
- pinch of salt and pepper
- 2 tbsp truffle oil
- 5 tbsp olive oil

How to make:

Whisk the ingredients in a bowl, saving the truffle oil and olive oil until last.

EXOTIC CHUTNEY DRESSING

Ingredients

- 2 tbsp mango chutney
- juice of fresh lime
- tspn ground cumin
- tspn salt
- 1/3 cup olive oil

How to make:

Whisk all the ingredients together. Make sure the oil goes in last and gradually.

BLUE CHEESE KICK

Ingredients

- 1/3 cup buttermilk
- 1/3 cup sour cream
- 100g crumbled blue cheese (use dolcelatte for vegetarian or check your cheese label!)
- juice ½ lemon
- pinch of salt and pepper

How to make:

Whisk all ingredients together in a blender for a creamy consistency.

HOT FIESTA DRESSING

Ingredients

- 5 chopped garlic cloves
- 1/3 cup olive oil
- juice of fresh lime
- juice of fresh orange
- 1 tspn ground cumin
- pinch of salt
- a handful of fresh chopped parsley

How to make:

- Firstly fry the garlic cloves on a medium heat in the olive oil for 1 minute (don't allow to brown)
- Now add the cooked garlic to a blender with the other ingredients (save the parsley for the end).
- Blend until smooth and add parsley before pulsing to mix.

EUROPEAN DRESSING

Ingredients

- 1/3 cup olive oil
- 1/3 cup water
- 2 tbsp red wine vinegar
- 1 tbsp tomato paste or puree
- 1 tbsp tomato ketchup
- 1 tbsp brown sugar
- pinch salt
- pinch paprika

How to make:

Whisk all the ingredients together in a food processer.

COUNTRY DRESSING

Ingredients

- ½ cup buttermilk
- ¼ cup mayonnaise
- handful of chopped parsley and chives
- 1 tbsp cider vinegar
- pinch of salt
- pinch of garlic powder
- 1 tbsp dried chilli flakes or fresh chilli

How to make:

Blend all the ingredients together in a food processer.

LIGHTER COUNTRY DRESSING

Ingredients

- ½ cup buttermilk
- ¼ cup mayonnaise
- ¼ cup natural yoghurt
- handful of chopped parsley and chives
- 1 tbsp cider vinegar
- pinch of salt
- pinch of garlic powder
- 1 tbsp dried chilli flakes or fresh chilli

How to make:

- Blend all the ingredients together in a food processer.

COUNTRY DRESSING WITH BACON

Ingredients

- ½ cup buttermilk
- ¼ cup mayonnaise
- handful of chopped parsley and chives
- 1 tbsp cider vinegar
- pinch of salt
- pinch of garlic powder
- 1 tbsp dried chilli flakes or fresh chilli
- 2 slices of bacon, cooked and chopped.

How to make:

- Blend all the ingredients together in a food processer.

COUNTRY AND WESTERN SMOKEY DRESSING

Ingredients

- ½ cup buttermilk
- ¼ cup mayonnaise
- Handful of chopped cilantro
- 1 tbsp cider vinegar
- Pinch of salt
- Pinch of garlic powder
- 1 tbsp dried chilli flakes or fresh chilli
- Chopped smoky chipotles

How to make:

- Blend all the ingredients together in a food processer.

CHOCOHOLIC'S DREAM DRESSING

Ingredients

- ¼ cup balsamic vinegar
- ¼ cup olive oil
- ¼ cup vegetable oil
- 3 tbsp cocoa powder (high quality)
- 1 tbsp caster sugar
- pinch of salt and pepper

How to make:

- Blend all of the ingredients and then add salt and pepper to taste. Goes deliciously with pear salads.

SWEET AND SAVOURY DRESSING

Ingredients

- 3 tbsp of mayonnaise
- 2 tbsp of cider vinegar
- Pinch of salt and pepper
- Handful of chopped and toasted walnuts

How to make:

- Whisk all the ingredients together by hand.

CREAMY GOAT'S CHEESE DRESSING

Ingredients

- 1/3 cup buttermilk
- 1/3 cup of softened goat's cheese
- 1 tbsp white wine vinegar
- 1 tbsp olive oil
- 1 tbsp horseradish
- Handful of chopped dill

How to make:

- Blend all the ingredients together in a food processer.

LOVELY LEMON DRESSING

Ingredients

- Juice and zest of 1 lemon
- 1 tbsp Dijon mustard
- Pinch of caster sugar and salt
- ¼ cup olive oil

How to make:

- Whisk all the ingredients together by hand.

LOVELY LEMON AND DILL DRESSING

Ingredients

- Juice and zest of 1 lemon
- 1 tbsp Dijon mustard
- Pinch of caster sugar and salt
- ¼ cup olive oil
- Handful of fresh chopped dill

How to make:

- Whisk all the ingredients together by hand.

LOVELY LEMON AND OLIVE DRESSING

Ingredients

- Juice and zest of 1 lemon
- 1 tbsp Dijon mustard
- Pinch of caster sugar and salt
- ¼ cup olive oil
- ¼ cup of pitted black olives
- Handful of fresh thyme

How to make:

- Whisk all the ingredients together by hand.

RED PEPPER DRESSING

Ingredients

- 3 chopped roasted red peppers (either from a jar or roasted at home in the oven)
- Handful of finely chopped fresh rosemary

How to make:

- Whisk all the ingredients together in a food processer.

HAZELNUT DELIGHT

Ingredients

- 2 tbsp Dijon mustard
- 2 tbsp cider vinegar
- A pinch of salt
- 1/3 cup olive oil
- 1/3 cup hazelnut oil (or fresh hazelnuts if available)
- Handful of fresh chives and dill

How to make:

- Blend the mustard and cider vinegar along with the salt and oils together to form a smooth dressing. Last add the herbs and pulse.

HERBY NUTTY DRESSING

Ingredients

- ½ cup olive oil
- Handful of toasted walnuts
- Juice of 1 fresh lemon
- A handful of fresh basil leaves
- ½ garlic clove
- Generous pinch of salt and pepper

How to make:

- Use a blender to combine all ingredients into a paste (some bits are fine to add texture!)

CITRUS DRESSING

Ingredients

- 2 tbsp balsamic vinegar
- Juice of fresh lemon
- 2 tbsp Dijon mustard
- Pinch of salt and pepper
- 4 tbsp olive oil
- Salt
- Pepper

How to make:

- Whisk all of the ingredients together, saving the olive oil to gradually add to form the consistency of your choice – thin for a lighter dressing.

BALSAMIC BLEND

Ingredients

- 2 tbsp balsamic vinegar
- Juice of fresh lemon
- 2 tbsp Dijon mustard
- Pinch of salt and pepper
- 4 tbsp olive oil
- Salt
- Pepper
- 2 tbsp mayonnaise
- ½ glove minced garlic
- tsp. sugar

How to make:

- Make the citrus dressing as above then add the mayonnaise, garlic and sugar for a creamier alternative!

SMOOTH ITALIAN

Ingredients

- 4 tbsp mayonnaise
- 2 tbsp red wine vinegar
- 2 tbsp sour cream
- 2 tbsp olive oil
- 1 tbsp dried Italian herbs
- ½ garlic clove
- Pinch of salt and pepper
- Handful of fresh chopped parsley
-

How to make:

- Use a blender or a whisk in a bowl to blend all of the ingredients, saving the fresh parsley for garnishing at the end.

RUSTIC RED ONION ITALIAN DRESSING

Ingredients

- Finely chopped red onion ½ (soak in cold water for 20 minutes)
- 1 chopped garlic clove
- Bunch of chopped fresh parsley
- tsp dried oregano
- Pinch of salt and black pepper
- 1 tbsp of olive oil
- 2 tbsp red wine vinegar

How to make:

- Add the garlic, herbs, salt and pepper and red onion onto a wooden board. Use a sharp knife to chop and blend into almost a paste. Now add the olive oil and red wine vinegar using your knife to mix. This forms a lovely base that you can pile your salad leaves on top of and mix around.

TROPICAL DRESSING

Ingredients

- 1 chopped and peeled mango
- 1 fresh lime (zest and juice)
- 1 tbsp Dijon mustard
- 1 tbsp caster sugar
- 1 tbsp salt
- 1/3 cup rice vinegar
- ½ cup olive oil

How to make:

- Puree all ingredients in a blender, gradually adding the rice vinegar and olive oil once the other ingredients have formed a smooth puree.

Printed in Great Britain
by Amazon